D1533751

First Facts™

Water All Around

Making Water Clean

by Rebecca Olien

Consultant:
Peter R. Jaffé, Professor
Department of Civil and Environmental Engineering
Princeton University
Princeton, New Jersey

press
Mankato, Minnesota

First Facts is published by Capstone Press,
151 Good Counsel Drive, P.O. Box 669, Mankato, Minnesota 56002.
www.capstonepress.com

Library of Congress Cataloging-in-Publication Data
Olien, Rebecca.
    Making water clean / by Rebecca Olien.
    p. cm.—(First facts. Water all around)
    Includes bibliographical references and index.
    ISBN 0-7368-3703-5 (hardcover)
    1. Water—Purification—Juvenile literature. I. Title. II. Series.
TD430.O43 2005
628.1'62—dc22   2004012232

Summary: Describes how cities treat freshwater so that it is safe to drink.

Editorial Credits
Christine Peterson, editor; Linda Clavel, designer; Ted Williams, illustrator; Kelly Garvin,
    photo researcher; Scott Thoms, photo editor

Photo Credits
Bruce Coleman Inc./E & P Bauer, 20
Corbis/PictureArts/Jack Andersen, cover
Gregg Andersen/Gallery 19, 5, 6, 7, 8, 10–11, 12–13, 14–15, 16, 19
Photo courtesy of Bolton & Menk Inc./Dennis Steele, 17

1 2 3 4 5 6 10 09 08 07 06 05

Table of Contents

Turn On the Faucet

Turn on the faucet and clear, clean water rushes out. People drink millions of glasses of clean water each day. But getting clean water to the faucet isn't as simple as it seems. Water goes through many steps before it becomes clean enough to drink.

Water Sources

Drinking water comes from many sources. Most cities get water from rivers and lakes.

Water seeps into the ground. It
collects in underground **aquifers**.
People dig wells to reach groundwater.

Safe Drinking Water

Most water in nature is not safe for people to drink. Rain washes dirt and waste into rivers. Materials from homes and farms **pollute** water sources.

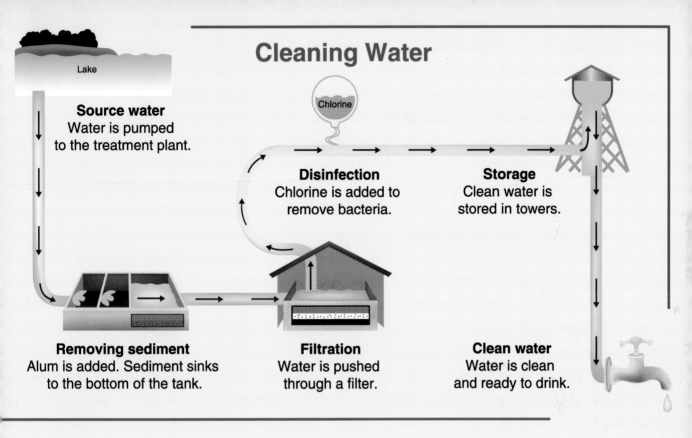

Cleaning Water

Lake

Source water
Water is pumped
to the treatment plant.

Chlorine

Disinfection
Chlorine is added to
remove bacteria.

Storage
Clean water is
stored in towers.

Removing sediment
Alum is added. Sediment sinks
to the bottom of the tank.

Filtration
Water is pushed
through a filter.

Clean water
Water is clean
and ready to drink.

Cities clean water to make it safe to drink. Dirt and other **particles** are taken out of the water. **Bacteria** that could make people sick are removed.

Pumping Water

Before water is treated, it must be pumped from a lake or river. Pumps also bring water up from under the ground.

In cities, pumps push water through miles (kilometers) of large pipes. The pipes carry water to treatment plants.

 Fact!
People who live outside cities get clean water from wells. Small particles are taken out as the water moves through the soil.

Removing Sediment

Treatment plants take out **sediment**. Sediment is dirt and particles found in water. A powder called alum is added to water to make the particles sticky.

The sticky particles sink to the bottom of tanks. Clear water is left on top. The water then is pushed through sand **filters** to take out any remaining particles.

Disinfection

Disinfection is the next step in making water clean. Treatment plants disinfect water by adding **chemicals** that kill bacteria. Most cities add chlorine to water. Water treated with chlorine protects people from disease.

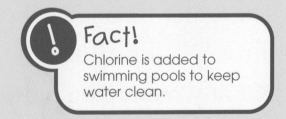

Fact!
Chlorine is added to swimming pools to keep water clean.

Moving Water

Once it is treated, water is ready for people to use. Clean water is pumped from the treatment plant to storage tanks. Many cities store water in large towers.

Water flows from towers through underground pipes called mains. Large water mains connect to smaller pipes. These pipes carry clean water to homes and businesses.

Clean Water

Communities use clean water in many ways. People need clean water to drink, cook, and clean. Cities make sure people have clean, safe water to use every day.

Fun Fact!
The United States and Canada have enough water pipes to circle the earth 40 times.

Amazing but True!

Beaver dams help keep water clean. Dams help make wetlands. Wetlands are filled with plants. Particles stick to plant roots and settle into the dirt. Water is cleaned as it flows through layers of roots and dirt.

Hands On: Cleaning Water

Water treatment plants remove sediment from water with alum. This experiment will show you how alum works.

What You Need

1 cup (240 mL) cold water

clear jar
1/2 teaspoon (2.5 mL) ground coffee
1 teaspoon (5 mL) flour

What You Do

1. Pour the cold water into the clear jar.
2. Add the ground coffee.
3. Look at the jar's side. Notice how the coffee floats on top of the water.
4. Sprinkle the flour into the jar.
5. Look through the jar's side to see what happens. The flour will form little clumps. As the clumps get heavier, they fall to the bottom of the jar bringing coffee grounds with them. Alum works the same way in water. Particles of dirt stick to the alum. The particles sink to the bottom of the tank.

Glossary

aquifer (AK-wuh-fuhr)—an underground lake

bacteria (bak-TIHR-ee-uh)—very small organisms; some bacteria cause disease.

chemical (KEM-uh-kuhl)—a substance that creates a reaction; chlorine is a chemical used to treat water.

disinfection (dis-in-FEKT-shuhn)—a process that kills harmful germs

filter (FIL-tur)—an object made of sand or gravel that removes particles from water

particle (PAR-tuh-kuhl)—a tiny piece of something

pollute (puh-LOOT)—to make something dirty or unsafe

sediment (SED-uh-muhnt)—bits of sand or clay carried by water or wind

Read More

Brunelle, Lynn. *Turn on the Faucet.* Step Back Science Series. San Diego: Blackbirch Press, 2004.

Kerley, Barbara. *A Cool Drink of Water.* Washington, D.C.: National Geographic Society, 2002.

Internet Sites

FactHound offers a safe, fun way to find Internet sites related to this book. All of the sites on FactHound have been researched by our staff.

Here's how:
1. Visit *www.facthound.com*
2. Type in this special code **0736837035** for age-appropriate sites. Or enter a search word related to this book for a more general search.
3. Click on the **Fetch It** button.

FactHound will fetch the best sites for you!

Index